GEMS
NATURE'S JEWELS
EMERALDS

By Eric Ethan

Gareth Stevens
Publishing

Please visit our Web site, www.garethstevens.com. For a free color catalog of all our high-quality books, call toll free 1-800-542-2595 or fax 1-877-542-2596.

For Michelle, a real gem.

Library of Congress Cataloging-in-Publication Data

Ethan, Eric.
  Emeralds / Eric Ethan.
    p. cm. — (Gems, nature's jewels)
  Includes index.
  ISBN 978-1-4339-4720-9 (pbk.)
  ISBN 978-1-4339-4721-6 (6-pack)
  ISBN 978-1-4339-4719-3 (lib. bdg.)
  1. Emeralds—Juvenile literature. 2. Mineralogy—Juvenile literature. I. Title.
  QE394.E5E84 2012
  553.8'6—dc22

                    2010031262

First Edition

Published in 2012 by
Gareth Stevens Publishing
111 East 14th Street, Suite 349
New York, NY 10003

Designer: Haley W. Harasymiw
Editor: Greg Roza

Photo credits: Cover, pp. 1, 4, 17, 21 Shutterstock.com; p. 5 Mark Ralston/AFP/Getty Images; pp. 6, 7 Mauricio Duenas/AFP/ Getty Images; p. 9 Mark Schneider/Visuals Unlimited/Getty Images; pp. 11, 12 Scott Dalton/Bloomberg via Getty Images; p. 13 David Boily/AFP/Getty Images; p. 15 Jan Sochor/Getty Images; p. 19 DAJ/Getty Images.

Printed in the United States of America

CPSIA compliance information: Batch #CS11GS: For further information contact Gareth Stevens, New York, New York at 1-800-542-2595.

CONTENTS

Words in the glossary appear in **bold** type the first time they are used in the text.

What Are Emeralds?

Emeralds are bright green, transparent crystals. "Transparent" means that you can see light shine through it. Emerald crystals form deep inside Earth as hot **magma** cools. They're made of a **mineral** called beryl. Pure beryl is clear and almost colorless. Emeralds get their bright green color from the element chromium, which mixes with the beryl as it cools.

It takes millions of years for emerald crystals to form. The oldest emeralds in the world are more than 2 **billion** years old!

GEM JOURNAL

The mineral beryl contains several elements, including beryllium, aluminum, and silicon.

Where Are Emeralds Found?

Emeralds were first mined in ancient Egypt over 4,000 years ago. Today, the finest emeralds come from Colombia, South America. Emerald mines near the Colombian cities of Muzo and Chivor are hundreds of years old. Inca Indians discovered these emerald **deposits** long before the Spanish arrived. Inca mines were very small.

The raw green emeralds shown here are still stuck in the rock in which they formed.

▼ This man is showing six raw Colombian emeralds.

The Spanish wanted more emeralds and dug many more tunnels. They used the Incas as slaves to dig them. These mines still produce a lot of gem-**quality** stones every year.

What Do Emeralds Look Like?

Emeralds come in many shades of green. The best ones are a deep grass green. They form deep inside the earth as six-sided crystals.

As the emerald crystals grow, other minerals often get trapped inside them. Bubbles of gas or liquid may also get trapped. These minerals and bubbles are called flaws or inclusions. Emeralds with many flaws are cloudy. The most **valuable** emeralds have few flaws and are very clear.

GEM JOURNAL

Emeralds from Colombia are a deep blue-green with few flaws. This makes them very valuable.

This gem-quality emerald crystal formed ▲
deep inside the earth long ago.

At the Mine

In some areas, miners dig deep tunnels to get emeralds out of the ground. It's hard, unsafe work. In the mine, emeralds can be hard to see, and it's easy to break them. Miners use hand tools to carefully dig through the rock and dirt. All the rock and dirt is taken to the surface in hand carts. Then it's carefully washed by miners looking for emeralds. Many carts of rock and dirt have to be removed to find one gem-quality stone.

A Colombian emerald mine worker pushes a cart full of dirt and rock to the surface.

Open-Pit Mining

The more common way people search for emeralds is called open-pit mining. Miners begin digging straight down, but they make the hole wider at the top. Open-pit mines have steep sides and can be very large. Many miners often work small pieces of land close to each other. This kind of mining needs a lot of water. The miners dig out a small amount of rock and dirt. Then they carefully wash it looking for emeralds.

A Colombian miner looks at a small emerald he has found in a large open-pit mine.

You can tell how big this open-pit mine is by looking at the trucks driving in and out of it.

GEM JOURNAL

Open-pit mines are often located near rivers or other large sources of water.

Making Emerald Jewelry

Gem-quality emerald crystals are cut and **polished** to make **jewelry**. Even though emerald is a hard stone, it can be split easily where it has inclusions.

Jewelers use a diamond saw and lots of water to cut the emerald crystal away from the rock it's found in. They go very slowly so that they don't damage the stone or cut away valuable crystal. The larger the finished emerald, the more valuable it will be.

GEM JOURNAL

Jewelers who cut and shape gems out of raw crystals are called lapidaries.

Here are five emeralds ready to be made ▲ into jewelry.

The Grinding Wheel

Lapidaries use wax to hold the raw emerald on a stick while they work on it. The lapidary holds the emerald against a **grinding wheel** and makes flat sides called facets around the stone. Facets have to be evenly spaced around the stone to make the finished gem sparkle. Emeralds are usually cut into square or rectangle shapes. Jewelers feel this shape best shows the color and sparkle of emeralds. This is sometimes called an emerald cut.

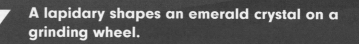

What Makes Emeralds Valuable?

An emerald's value is based on its cut, color, and **clarity**. Most emeralds are cut in a square shape. If the facets are all evenly spaced, an emerald will sparkle with a color jewelers call "green fire." The fewer flaws an emerald has, the easier it is to see through it. This gives the emerald a high level of clarity.

Emeralds are actually more valuable than diamonds of the same weight. Flawless emeralds are the most expensive gems in the world.

GEM JOURNAL

A unit called the carat is used to weigh gems. Five carats are equal to 1 gram (0.035 oz).

This is a very valuable set of emerald and diamond jewelry.

Really Rare Emeralds

The Mogul Emerald is more than 300 years old. It belonged to a ruler of India. It's cut into a rectangle, and it's nearly 4 inches (10 cm) long. One side has prayers **etched** on it.

The Gachala Emerald is one of the largest uncut emeralds in the world. It weighs over 850 carats! Originally from Colombia, it's now kept at the Smithsonian Institution in Washington, D.C.

The Hooker Emerald **Brooch** is made of one of the most flawless emeralds ever found.

The Emerald Mine

- Emerald mining is described in the oldest book in the world, which is called the Papyrus Prisse.

- Emerald is the birthstone for the month of May.

- People began creating man-made emeralds in the 1960s.

- Man-made emeralds are easy to spot because they're perfect and have no flaws like natural emeralds do.

- Long ago, emerald was thought to cure poison.

- Emeralds are a symbol of everlasting life.

- The process of treating poor-quality emeralds with cedar wood oil to improve their appearance began with the ancient Greeks.

Glossary

billion: 1,000 million, or 1,000,000,000

brooch: a piece of jewelry that can be pinned to clothing

clarity: the state of being clear

deposit: an amount of a mineral in the ground that built up over a period of time

etch: to cut words or shapes into a hard surface

grinding wheel: a wheel with a rough surface, used to shape or smooth a gem

jewelry: pieces of metal, often holding gems, worn on the body

magma: hot, liquid rock inside Earth

mineral: matter in the ground that forms rocks

polish: to make something smooth and shiny by rubbing it with a soft cloth

quality: the standard or grade of something

valuable: worth a lot of money

For More Information

Books

Petersen, Christine. *Groovy Gems*. Edina, MN: ABDO Publishing, 2010.

Symes, R. F., and R. R. Harding. *Crystal and Gem*. New York, NY: DK Publishing, 2007.

Web Sites

The Dynamic Earth
www.mnh.si.edu/earth/text
Explore gems, minerals, and mining at the National Museum of Natural History Web site.

The Mineral and Gemstone Kingdom
www.minerals.net
Read about gems and minerals.

Index